BEGIN READING TODAY

A Fun and Simple Approach
to Reading 50 Sight Words

Heidi Unkrich

Hardback ISBN: 978-1-7345707-1-7

Paperback ISBN: 978-1-7345707-0-0

Library of Congress Control Number: 2020903532

Book Design by Talitha Shipman

Images provided by StockUnlimited and Adobe Stock

Cover icons created by Freepic on www.flaticon.com

Foundations for Learning Publishing

www.beginreadingtoday.com

Dedicated to all the children who want to begin reading today

Table of Contents

Preface 9

General Information 10

How to Use This Book 10

Correcting Reading Errors 11

Alternative Method for Struggling Readers 13

Special Note for You 14

Another Special Note for You 14

Progress Page Information 14

Progress Page 15

A 18

And 20

See 22

The 24

Go 26

I 28

In 30

To 32

Is 34

You 36

For 38

It and the Question Mark 40

He 42

Look 44

At 46

Up 48

His 50

She 52

That 54

Was 56

On 58

They 60

Said 62

With 64

Had 66

Halfway Mark and Instructions 68

All 69

Have 70

Do 71

Can 72

We 73

Be 74

Of 75

Not 76

There 77

What 78

This 79

But 80

Are 81

When 82

One 83

Out and the Exclamation Mark 84

Him 85

Some 86

As 87

Were 88

Her 89

Then 90

Will 91

So 92

From 93

Stories and Practice 94

Acknowledgements 99

Preface

When children are ready to read, they want to be able to pick up a book and begin reading right away. As a mother of two and a reading tutor, I struggled to find books for these eager readers. Usually discouragement would set in as the reader tried to sound out and recognize sight words. Losing confidence or interest, the reader would quickly give up the idea of picking up a book to read again anytime soon.

Many parents or caretakers want to help with reading but think because they are not a teacher, they do not have the skills. Or, like me, they cannot find any books the eager reader can begin reading right away.

After 20 years of tutoring in reading, I set out to write a reading book in which the discouragement level for the reader would be low, and the feelings of success would be high. Each page introduces only one new sight word and is full of colorful pictures to aid in the enjoyment of learning. Because each new sight word is introduced and reinforced in a systematic, thoughtful way beginning with the easiest, most frequent sight words, the eager reader can read through the book at his or her own pace and complete it mastering 50 sight words.

I continue to teach phonics, so I do not in any way diminish the value of phonics, which is a much-needed skill in reading and spelling. Knowing sight words simply aids in learning how to read and is a great foundation because, simply put, not all words are spelled phonetically.

This book is for the eager reader but is most certainly for the reluctant reader, as well. In fact, most reluctant readers began as eager readers but became discouraged. Whether you have an eager reader or a reluctant reader, this book will be a great resource for developing a foundation and a love for reading.

General Information

The reader needs to know the upper and lower-case letters of the alphabet before beginning.

Understand that if this is the very first time your reader has ever read, then the reader is not only learning to read words, the reader is learning to read from left to right and to read *every single word* as it comes up on the line. You will need to point to each word in a sentence or line until your reader gets used to reading from left to right. We take many things for granted because we have been reading for so long. Your reader will quickly be taking this new concept for granted, as well.

An index card or a bookmark is needed to be placed under each line being read. An index card folded in half works well because it is smaller, easier to manage, and almost always accessible.

How much time Should be Spent Reading?

The amount of time to be spent each day on reading depends on the age and attention span of the reader. Generally speaking, age times two to three minutes per day works well. (Five years old = 5 x 2 to 3 minutes = 10 to 15 minutes per day.) This is not a hard-fast rule. Use your best judgement. Discontinue the lesson if your reader becomes weary; continue if enthusiasm is still high. The goal is to develop a *love* of reading, not a dread of reading.

Choose a time for lessons when your reader feels good! If your reader is a morning person, have lessons then. If your reader feels better after lunch, have lessons then. Do not have lessons at a time when your reader is tired or stressed.

If the reader is having difficulty with a particular page, take a break and begin again the next day. A break is good for the brain. When I first began teaching, I had this noble idea that I would never give up on a child; I would teach, teach, teach until understanding took place. Wrong. A more effective way is to take a break when frustration has set in and begin again the next day. You and the reader will be amazed at how much easier everything seems.

How to Use This Book

This book follows a fun and simple approach to teaching sight words. Only one sight word is introduced at a time. The reader will read the new sight word 10 times on the first page and then read lines or sentences containing that sight word on the next page. The sentence page will be read several times until the reader can read the whole page with three or less errors. When the sentence page has been read with three or less errors, the reader is ready to be introduced to another sight word, and the process repeats.

Most pages have the same specific instructions; however, occasionally new information or instructions will be introduced. These will be identified by a **Special Note**.

The use of pictures for words is used in this ◆ to aid in writing sentences and to add fun to the reading. Readers enjoy seeing and identifying the colorful pictures. The word for each picture is not given because identifying the exact word for the picture is not the primary purpose. If the reader calls a picture of a dog "puppy" or reads "sandwich" for hamburger, gently correct him or her as you deem necessary. Everyday, ordinary objects have been used for the pictures; however, your reader may not be able to identify some of the pictures, such as a panda or a penguin. This will be an opportunity to tell the reader what that object is, and the reader's increased vocabulary will be a bonus.

My reader already knows a few sight words. Where do I begin?

If your reader already knows a few sight words, you can save time by asking him or her to read the new sight word on each page. If your reader reads it correctly, have the reader pick out three sentences on the sentence page to read. If these are read correctly, continue to the next new sight word page and repeat the process until you come to a word the reader cannot read.

Make sure to read the instructions and tips on each new sight word page even if your reader already knows the sight word.

Correcting Reading Errors

Resist the urge to correct your reader right away. A reader will sometimes make a correction, but he or she will not have a chance to do that if the correction is quickly being made by you. When your reader corrects a mistake, give encouragement by saying something like, "Good job on caching that!"

How do I Correct my Reader?

When the reader does read a word incorrectly, point to the word, read it correctly and have the reader read that word. Ask the reader to start from the beginning of the sentence and reread. If the reader makes another mistake in the sentence, again point to the word, read it correctly and have the reader read the word to you before rereading the sentence. Move on to the next sentence after the third correction. Spending too much time on one sentence can cause frustration. Most likely, your reader will have a chance to read that sentence again.

Example from a sentence on page 39:

Go to the for a .

Reader: "Go to the table *from....*"
You: (Point to *for*) "This word is '*for*.' Say it."
Reader: "For."
You: "Let's try that sentence again."
Reader: "Go to the table *for* a donut."
You: "Ok, good job."

In addition, your reader should not *add* words to the sentences.

Example from another sentence on page 39:

Go to the for and the .

Reader: "Go to the crib for *the* baby and the pacifier.
You: "There is no *the* before baby – it's just *for baby*."
Reader: "Go to the crib *for baby* and the pacifier."
You: "Yes, that's right."

Adding Variety when Rereading the Sentence Page

Because the sentence page may have to be read several times for mastery to take place, you can add variety by having the reader start at the bottom and read up after the page has been read from top to bottom once. Next time allow the reader to pick out five sentences to read, and then you can pick out the rest until the whole page is read. Readers enjoy picking out sentences to read. Another option is to read every other sentence until all sentences have been read. (Mastery is when the reader has made three or less errors on a page.)

A Particular Page is Causing Frustration. What Should I Do?

Occasionally, a particular page might cause a reader frustration, or too much time has been spent on one page. If this happens, now is the time to stop the lesson and begin again on another day.

If the reader continues to make two to three mistakes per sentence and is struggling with reading the sentences correctly, go back three to six pages and begin that page with the sight word. Or if a particular sight word prevents your reader from mastering a sentence page, go back to the page that sight word was introduced and go through the reading practice again. A review is highly effective for correction and getting the reader back on track.

The number of pages read is not as important as mastering the pages read.

This book enables you to guide the reader at his or her own pace. Some readers may read one page a day; others may read two to five pages a day. If you rush the reader through the pages and skip over the steps, the reader will begin to struggle. Follow the steps and go at your reader's own pace. Read and have fun!

Alternative Method for Struggling Readers

After having introduced the new sight word and your reader having read the new words on both pages, follow these steps:

1. Place the bookmark or index card under the first sentence and point to each word and image as you read the sentence.

2. Ask the reader to read the sentence you just read.

3. Repeat these steps for the next four sentences.

4. Ask the reader to read the first five sentences without your having read them first.

5. Read sentence six pointing to each word and image.

6. Ask the reader to read sentence six to you.

7. Repeat for sentences seven through ten.

8. Ask the reader to read sentences six through ten without your having read them first.

9. Finally, have the reader read the whole page to you. Correct as usual when needed.

10. If three or less errors are made, continue to the next page and repeat the same process.

After using this method for a few pages, try to use the standard approach given previously for the next sight word.

If your reader is having great difficulty with reading, it could be that the reader is young and not quite ready to read. Taking a break of three to six months can make all the difference.

Special Note for You

Reading books to children is a perfect way to develop a love of reading. Ask questions about the story or pictures in the book to enhance reading comprehension. Go to the library once a week and allow children to pick out a few books along with the books you pick out for them. Let children see you reading books. Have a time set aside every day for reading. If possible, extend bedtime by 10 minutes and designate it "reading time," or decide that 15 minutes *before* bedtime is Book Time! Turn off the television and electronics as much as possible.

Another Special Note Just for You

You know your reader better than I do. These are recommendations I have learned through the years of working with students, but if something else works for your reader that I have not mentioned here, great! We all learn at different paces, and different methods work better for some and not for others. If you try something new that works, or if you have any questions, I would love to hear from you at heidi@ beginreadingtoday.com.

Progress Page Instructions

A Progress Page is provided for your reader. You and your reader can set a goal to read this book every day, two to five days a week, or whatever you decide. A reward after every five to ten pages completed can also be set up. If possible, allow your reader to choose the reward.

The Progress Page may be duplicated. Place it in a location for your reader to see and have easy access to for placing stickers or for marking off sight words mastered.

This visual Progress Page will be a real encouragement to your reader. Everyone likes to see progress, and everyone likes rewards!

PROGRESS PLAN FOR _____

I will read ____ days a week.

After ____ pages are completed,

_____

_____

When the whole book is completed,

_____

_____

○ A	○ She	○ What
○ And	○ That	○ This
○ See	○ Was	○ But
○ The	○ On	○ Are
○ Go	○ They	○ When
○ I	○ Said	○ One
○ In	○ With	○ Out
○ To	○ Had	○ Him
○ Is	○ All	○ Some
○ You	○ Have	○ As
○ For	○ Do	○ Were
○ It	○ Can	○ Her
○ He	○ We	○ Then
○ Look	○ Be	○ Will
○ At	○ Of	○ So
○ Up	○ Not	○ From
○ His	○ There	

PROGRESS PLAN FOR_____

I will read ____ days a week.

After ____ pages are completed,

_____

_____

When the whole book is completed,

_____

_____

○ A	○ She	○ What
○ And	○ That	○ This
○ See	○ Was	○ But
○ The	○ On	○ Are
○ Go	○ They	○ When
○ I	○ Said	○ One
○ In	○ With	○ Out
○ To	○ Had	○ Him
○ Is	○ All	○ Some
○ You	○ Have	○ As
○ For	○ Do	○ Were
○ It	○ Can	○ Her
○ He	○ We	○ Then
○ Look	○ Be	○ Will
○ At	○ Of	○ So
○ Up	○ Not	○ From
○ His	○ There	

This page may be reproduced.

Let's Begin Reading!

A

We begin with the letter A which is a sight word! Point to the first letter A below and say, "This is the capital letter A which is a sight word." Now point to the lower-case a and say, "This is also a sight word that uses a lower-case a."

Point out to your reader that we read from left to right. Or simply put for the younger reader, we start on this side of the page which is left (point to it) and read to this side of the page which is right (point to it). For the beginning reader, this is important information he or she might not realize but will quickly grasp.

Now have the reader use the index card and read the letter A's below from left to right. When the reader has read all 10 A's successfully, continue to the next instruction below.

A	a
A	a
a	A
a	A
a	A

On the next page, your reader will place the index card under the first line and begin reading the letter A with the picture. You may need to move the index card down for now. When the page has been read with three or less errors made, your reader is ready to continue to the next new sight word.

Perfection in saying the absolute correct word for the picture isn't the primary emphasis. Correct as needed.
Give lots of encouragement: Good work! Wow. Well done. Nice!

Refer to pages 11 and 12 for tips on correcting and/or repeating a page.

A

A

A

A

A

A

A

A

A

A

And

This page introduces the word *and*. Point to the *and* below and say, "This is the word *and*." Also point out that one *And* begins with a capital *A* and the one beside it begins with a lower-case *a*. Now have the reader use the index card and read the list below from left to right.

And	and
And	and
and	And
and	And
And	and

On the next page your reader will place the index card under the first line and begin reading. You may need to move the index card down. When the page has been read with three or less errors made, your reader is ready to continue to the next new sight word.

Remember perfection in saying the absolute correct word for the picture is not the primary emphasis. Correct as needed.

Resist the urge to correct your reader right away. A reader will sometimes self-correct, but he or she will not have a chance to do that if you are quickly making the correction. Encourage your reader when self-correction happens by saying, "Good job on catching that!"

Refer to pages 11 and 12 for tips on correcting and/or repeating a page.

A  and a

A and a

A and a

A and a

A and a

A and a

A and a

A and a

A and a

A  and a

See

Congratulations! By now your reader knows two sight words and is ready to read a simple sentence. The next word is *see*, and you will do the same thing you have done with *a* and *and*: Point to the word and say, "*see*." Point out the upper and lower-case letter *S* as needed. Now have the reader read the words on this page from left to right using the index card.

See	see
See	See
see	see
See	see
see	See

Special Note: After your reader has successfully read *see*, let your reader know that *sentences* will be read from now on, and at the end of every sentence is a period. Point to the first five periods on the next page, and have your reader point out the last five periods. The first two pages read were not sentences and did not have periods. From now on sentences will be read.

On the next page, your reader will place the index card under the first sentence and begin reading. When the page has been read with three or less errors made, your reader is ready to continue to the next new sight word.

Your reader is not expected to read through the sentence page perfectly the first time. The sentence page may need to be read several times for mastery. Give lots of praise and encouragement!

Refer to pages 11 and 12 for tips on correcting and/or repeating a page.

23

See a  .

See a .

See a .

See a .

See a and a .

See a and a .

See a and a .

See a and a .

See a and a .

See a and a .

The

This page introduces the word *the*. Point to *the* below and say, "This is the word *the*." Point out the upper and lower-case letter *T* as needed. Now have the reader read the words on this page from left to right using the index card.

The	the
The	the
the	The
the	the
The	The

Special note: The word *sees* is also on this page. Let your reader know that *sees* is just like *see* except there is an *s* at the end. Here is a little practice with both of these words:

Sees	sees
See	See
See	sees
sees	see
sees	Sees

On the next page, your reader will place the index card under the first sentence and begin reading. When the page has been read with three or less errors made, your reader is ready to continue to the next new sight-word.

When you begin reading on another day, start on the previous sentence page — this will serve as a great review.

Refer to pages 11 and 12 for tips on correcting and/or repeating a page.

25

The 🧒 sees the ✈️ .

The 🐕 and 🐈 see the ⚽ .

The 👩‍⚕️ sees the 🧸 .

The 👶 sees the 🗼 and the 🧱 .

The 👨‍🌾 sees a 🚜 and a 🏚️ .

The 👦 and 👧 see the 🛹 .

The 👵 sees the 👓 and a ✏️ .

The 👩 and 👦 see a 🎁 .

The 🧑 sees a 🎒 and a 📙 .

The 2 🐦 🐦 see a 🪺 .

Go

This page introduces the word *go*. Point to *go* below and say, "This is the word *go*." Point out the upper and lower-case letter *G* as needed. Now have the reader read the words on this page from left to right using the index card.

Go	go
Go	Go
go	go
Go	Go
go	go

Special note: Because the sentences are getting longer, now is a good time for the reader to start locating the new sight words on the sentence page *before* reading it. Readers enjoy finding the new words, pointing to them, and reading them out loud. Have the reader point to and read out loud each *go* on the next page before reading the sentences.

Encourage your reader to use the index card on his or her own.

On the next page, your reader will place the index card under the first sentence and begin reading. When the page has been read with three or less errors made, your reader is ready to continue to the next new sight word.

When your reader is rereading a page, add variety by allowing your reader to pick out five sentences to read — then you pick out the remaining five.

Words of encouragement: Amazing. You're doing such a good job!

Refer to pages 11 and 12 for tips on correcting and/or repeating a page.

Go see the .

Go see the .

Go see the .

Go see the and the .

Go see a and a .

Go see the and the .

Go see the and the .

Go see a and a .

Go see the and the .

The and go and see the .

I

This page introduces the word *I*. Point to *I* and say, "This is the word *I*. This letter *I* is a sight word like the letter *A*." Special note for your reader: the letter I is always capitalized when it is a sight word, but not always when it is part of a regular word. Have the reader use the index card and read the list below left to right.

I	I
I	I
I	I
I	I
I	I

Special Note: The next page contains three sentences that have a comma in them. Point to them. Tell your reader that these commas join two sentences together with the word *and*. You are only introducing your reader to these punctuation concepts; do not worry if the reader does not completely understand at this time. The reader is simply becoming aware of written language and punctuation that is used.

Have the reader point to and read out loud each *I* on the next page before reading the sentences.

On the next page, your reader will place the index card under the first sentence and begin reading. When the page has been read with three or less errors made, your reader is ready to continue to the next new sight word

Your reader should not add words to sentences.
This counts as an error.

Refer to pages 11 and 12 for tips on correcting and/or repeating a page.

I go see the .

I go see the .

I go and see a .

I see a , and I go.

The and I see the .

The and I see the .

The sees a , and I see a .

The sees a , and I see a .

I go and see the .

I go and see the .

In

This page introduces the word *in*. Point to *in* below and say, "This is the word *in*." Point out the upper and lower-case letter *I* as needed. Now have the reader read the words on this page from left to right using the index card.

In	in
In	In
In	in
in	In
in	in

Have the reader point to and read out loud each *in* on the next page before reading the sentences.

On the next page, your reader will place the index card under the first sentence and begin reading. When the page has been read with three or less errors made, your reader is ready to continue to the next new sight word.

The number of pages read is not as important as mastering the pages read. Don't skip the steps or rush the process. Go at your reader's own pace. Let the reader check off or place a sticker next to the sight word mastered on the Progress Plan.

Refer to pages 11 and 12 for tips on correcting and/or repeating a page.

I see in the .

I see in the .

I see a in the .

I see a go in the .

See the go in the .

See the go in the .

See the and in the .

See the and in the .

See a and a in the .

See the and a in the .

To

This page introduces the word *to*. Point to *to* below and say, "This is the word *to*." Point out the upper and lower-case letter *T* as needed. Now have the reader read the words on this page from left to right using the index card.

To	to
To	To
to	to
To	To
to	to

Have the reader point to and read out loud each *to* on the next page before reading the sentences.

On the next page, your reader will place the index card under the first sentence and begin reading. When the page has been read with three or less errors made, your reader is ready to continue to the next new sight word.

Another way to add variety when rereading the sentence page a second time is to have your reader read every other sentence — then go back and read the ones skipped.

Refer to pages 11 and 12 for tips on correcting and/or repeating a page.

Go to  .

Go to the 🪟 .

Go to see the 🚂 .

I go in to see the 🐼 and the 🦒 .

I go in to see the 🎄 and 🎁 .

I go in to see a 🕐 .

The 👦 and 👧 go to the 🚌 .

Go in the 🏠 to see the 🎂 .

See the 🐄 go to a 🛖 .

See the 👶 go to a ⚪ .

Is

This page introduces the word *is*. Point to *is* below and say, "This is the word *is*." Point out the upper and lower-case letter *I* as needed. Now have the reader read the words on this page from left to right using the index card.

Is	is
Is	is
is	is
Is	Is
Is	is

Have the reader point to and read out loud each *is* on the next page before reading the sentences.

On the next page, your reader will place the index card under the first sentence and begin reading. When the page has been read with three or less errors made, your reader is ready to continue to the next new sight word.

Do you have a designated "reading time"?
Good habits need to be cultivated.
Do your children see you reading?

Refer to pages 11 and 12 for tips on correcting and/or repeating a page.

The  is in the .

The is in the .

The is in the .

I go and see the is in a .

I go to see the is in a .

The sees the is in the .

I go and see the is in the .

The is in a to see .

The is in a to see the .

The is in a to see a .

You

This page introduces the word *you*. Point to *you* below and say, "This is the word *you*." Point out the upper and lower-case letter *Y* as needed. Now have the reader read the words on this page from left to right using the index card.

You   you

You   you

you   You

You   you

you   You

Have the reader point to and read out loud each *you* on the next page before reading the sentences.

On the next page, your reader will place the index card under the first sentence and begin reading. When the page has been read with three or less errors made, your reader is ready to continue to the next new sight word.

If your reader has reread a sentence page several times and is still struggling, stop and begin another day a couple pages back. A break works wonders for more than just reading.

Refer to pages 11 and 12 for tips on correcting and/or repeating a page.

You go in the .

You go in the  .

You and I go to the  .

You and I go to a .

You see the and the .

You see the and go to .

You see the is in the .

You see a is in the .

The sees you go in the .

You and I go to the  to see the .

For

This page introduces the word *for*. Point to *for* below and say, "This is the word *for*." Point out the upper and lower-case letter *F* as needed. Now have the reader read the words on this page from left to right using the index card.

For	for
for	For
For	for
for	for
For	For

Have the reader point to and read out loud each *for* on the next page.

Next, your reader will place the index card under the first sentence and begin reading. When the page has been read with three or less errors made, your reader is ready to continue to the next new sight word.

Spending too much time on one sentence can cause frustration. Don't read the same sentence more than three times. Most likely, your reader will have a chance to read that sentence again.

Refer to pages 11 and 12 for tips on correcting and/or repeating a page.

The ⬭ is for you.

The ✿ is for you.

The ☂ is for you and the 👧.

A 🛋 is for the ⬛.

I see a 🏀 is for the 🏀.

I see the 🐕 for you is in the 🚗.

The 👦 sees the 🍦 in the 🗄 for you.

Go to the 🪑 for a 🍩.

Go to the 🛏 for 👶 and the ⌀.

Go in the 🏠 for 🕶 and a 🧥.

It

This page introduces the word *it*. Point to *it* below and say, "This is the word *it*." Point out the upper and lower-case letter *I* as needed. Now have the reader read the words on this page from left to right using the index card.

It	it
It	It
it	it
It	It
it	it

Special note: The question mark is introduced on the next page. Point to the question mark and say, "This is a question mark. The question mark goes at the end of the sentence that is a question." You can then give an example of a question and ask your reader to think of a question. Let the reader know that we read a question differently than we do a statement. From now on, whenever a question is read, ensure that your reader is reading it as a question and not a statement.

Another special note: The next page also contains lines that have two sentences instead of only one. Point out the lines that have two sentences to your reader. Explain to your reader the first sentence ends in a period because it is simply a statement, and the second one ends in a question mark because it is a question. Also point out that after the period is a slight pause before beginning the next sentence.

Have the reader point to and read out loud each *it* on the next page. Also have the reader point to all the question marks.

On the next page, your reader will place the index card under the first sentence and begin reading. When the page has been read with three or less errors made, your reader is ready to continue to the next sight word.

Refer to pages 11 and 12 for tips on correcting and/or repeating a page.

Is it in a ?

Is it a 🐼?

Is it in the 🏠?

Is it for the 🐶?

I see the 💍. Is it for you?

I see the 🍕. Is it for you?

The 👧 sees the 🥣. Is it for a 🐱?

Go to a 🏚. Is a 🐓 in it?

Is it a 🍓🧁?

Go to the 🎄 and see it. Is the 🎁 for you?

He

This page introduces the word *he*. Point to *he* below and say, "This is the word *he*." Point out the upper and lower-case letter *H* as needed. Now have the reader read the words on this page from left to right using the index card.

He	he
he	He
he	He
He	he
he	He

Special Note: Continue to encourage your reader to read the interrogative (question) statements as a question and not a statement. *Almost* every page will have a question mark on it somewhere.

Have your reader point to and read out loud each *he* on the next page.

Next, your reader will place the index card under the first sentence and begin reading. When the page has been read with three or less errors made, your reader is ready to continue to the next new sight word.

Remember: It is normal for your reader to read the page several times before mastery takes place! Learning is taking place. There is no such thing as fast-food education.

Refer to pages 11 and 12 for tips on correcting and/or repeating a page.

He is in the  .

He is in the .

Is he a  ?

Is he a ?

I see he is .

He sees the for it.

He sees  for the .

He and I go to the for it.

You and he go to the for a .

You and he go to see the .

Look

This page introduces the word *look*. Point to *look* below and say, "This is the word *look*." Point out the upper and lower-case letter *L* as needed. Now have the reader read the words on this page from left to right using the index card.

Look   look

look   Look

Look   look

look   Look

Look   look

Special note: The word *looks* is also on this page. Here's a little practice.

Looks   looks

Looks   Looks

looks   looks

looks   Looks

Looks   looks

Have your reader point to and read out loud each *look* and *looks* on the next page.

Next, your reader will place the index card under the first sentence and begin reading. When the page has been read with three or less errors made, your reader is ready to continue to the next new sight word.

Refer to pages 11 and 12 for tips on correcting and/or repeating a page.

Look for a .

You look for the .

You look for the .

Look, is he the ?

He looks in a for it.

He looks and sees it in the  .

I go to look for the .

He and I look for .

Look, is a in the ?

Go to look for the .

At

This page introduces the word *at*. Point to *at* below and say, "This is the word *at*." Point out the upper and lower-case letter *A* as needed. Now have the reader read the words on this page from left to right using the index card.

At	at
at	At
At	at
At	at
at	At

Have your reader point to and read out loud each *at* on the next page.

Next, your reader will place the index card under the first sentence and begin reading. When the page has been read with three or less errors made, your reader is ready to continue to the next new sight word.

By now your reader has learned many new sight words. If your reader is not enjoying the reading as much or is struggling, go back three to five sight words and pick up the lessons there. Sometimes a review is needed to boost confidence.

Refer to pages 11 and 12 for tips on correcting and/or repeating a page.

Look at the 🌰 for the 🐿️.

It is a 🧒 at the 🚪.

I look at a 🎁 for the 👧.

You and he look at a 🎂.

You and he look at the 🍞 in the 🔥.

Look at the 📺 and see a ⚽.

Go and look for the ⚪ at the 🛝.

Is it in a 🗄️ at the 🏠?

Go to the 🛋️ and look at the 🥁.

I go to the 🛏️ to look at the 👶.

Up

This page introduces the word *up*. Point to *up* below and say, "This is the word *up*." Point out the upper and lower-case letter *U* as needed. Now have the reader read the words on this page from left to right using the index card.

Up	up
up	Up
Up	up
up	Up
up	Up

Have your reader point to and read out loud each *up* on the next page.

Special Note: The next page contains lines with two sentences in them. Make sure the reader is pausing slightly at the period and not reading the line as one sentence.

On the next page, your reader will place the index card under the first sentence and begin reading. When the page has been read with three or less errors made, your reader is ready to continue to the next new sight word.

When a new day of reading begins, start with the last sentence page read ~ this serves as a terrific review.

Refer to pages 11 and 12 for tips on correcting and/or repeating a page.

You go up the .

Go up to the and see the .

Go up to see the for you.

Look at the go up. It is in a .

Look at the go up. It is in a .

He and I see the go up.

The sees the go up.

Is the up in the ?

Is he up in the ?

Look up at the . It is for you.

His

This page introduces the word *his*. Point to *his* below and say, "This is the word *his*." Point out the upper and lower-case letter *H* as needed. Now have the reader read the words on this page from left to right using the index card.

His   his

His   his

his   His

his   His

His   his

Have your reader point to and read out loud each *his* on the next page.

Next, your reader will place the index card under the first sentence and begin reading. When the page has been read with three or less errors made, your reader is ready to continue to the next new sight word.

Resist the urge to correct right away.

Encouraging words: Look how many words you know already!
I like hearing you read! Good work.

Refer to pages 11 and 12 for tips on correcting and/or repeating a page.

Is it his 🧢 ?

His 🦆 is in the 🛁 .

His 🐕 is in a 🚚 .

I see his 👖 and his 🧥 .

He sees his 🍕 in the ▭ .

He sees his 🏀 go in the 🏀🥅 .

You look for his 🕶️ and his 🏐 .

Go to the 🛖 and look at his 🐷 .

The 👶 looks up for his 🍼 .

The 🧒 looks up at his 🕐 .

She

This page introduces the word *she*. Point to *she* below and say, "This is the word *she*." Point out the upper and lower-case letter *S* as needed. Now have the reader read the words on this page from left to right using the index card.

She	she
She	she
she	She
she	she
She	She

Have your reader point to and read out loud each *she* on the next page.

Next, your reader will place the index card under the first sentence and begin reading. When the page has been read with three or less errors made, your reader is ready to continue to the next new sight word.

Have you been to the library this week?
Children love choosing their own books.
It's empowering!

Refer to pages 11 and 12 for tips on correcting and/or repeating a page.

53

She looks at his .

She and I look at his .

She looks up at the in his .

You and she go up in the  .

He and she go to the .

You and she see for the .

She sees it is a for .

He and she see it is in a .

Is she in the ?

Is she in a to see the ?

That

This page introduces the word *that*. Point to *that* below and say, "This is the word *that*." Point out the upper and lower-case letter *T* as needed. Now have the reader read the words on this page from left to right using the index card.

That   that

That   that

that   That

that   that

That   That

Have your reader point to and read out loud each *that* on the next page.

Next, your reader will place the index card under the first sentence and begin reading. When the page has been read with three or less errors made, your reader is ready to continue to the next new sight word.

Has your reader seen you enjoying a good book lately?

Refer to pages 11 and 12 for tips on correcting and/or repeating a page.

Look up at that .

The is in that .

She and I look up at that .

Is that for you?

Go to look for his in that .

She looks at that .

Is it a that he sees?

Go to that for his .

She looks for his  in that .

He sees that for you.

Was

This page introduces the word *was*. Point to *was* below and say, "This is the word *was*." Point out the upper and lower-case letter *W* as needed. Now have the reader read the words on this page from left to right using the index card.

Was	was
was	was
Was	Was
was	Was
was	Was

Have your reader point to and read out loud each *was* on the next page.

Next, your reader will place the index card under the first sentence and begin reading. When the page has been read with three or less errors made, your reader is ready to continue to the next new sight word.

The goal is to develop a love of reading.

Refer to pages 11 and 12 for tips on correcting and/or repeating a page.

He was a in the .

She was in the .

The was for the .

I see he was in his .

A was in that .

Was that for you and the ?

Was it in his ?

I go to a that was up in a .

Is that the that was for the ?

She looks up at his that was

in the .

On

This page introduces the word *on*. Point to *on* below and say, "This is the word *on*." Point out the upper and lower-case letter *O* as needed. Now have the reader read the words on this page from left to right using the index card.

On	on
On	On
on	on
on	on
On	On

Have your reader point to and read out loud each *on* on the next page.

Next, your reader will place the index card under the first sentence and begin reading. When the page has been read with three or less errors made, your reader is ready to continue to the next new sight word.

When rereading the sentence page, add variety by starting at the bottom of the page and reading up.

Refer to pages 11 and 12 for tips on correcting and/or repeating a page.

She is on the 🛴.

She was on the 🚲.

Was that 🐕 on the 🛋️?

I see the 🥞 on the 🪑.

It is up on his 📚.

You and she go on a 🏍️.

He looks for his 👕 on the 🪑.

Look up at that 🐝 on the 🌻.

Go on a ⛵ to see 🐟.

Was that 🧒 on his 🛹 in the 🏠?

They

This page introduces the word *they*. Point to *they* below and say, "This is the word *they*." Point out the upper and lower-case letter *T* as needed. Now have the reader read the words on this page from left to right using the index card.

They   they

They   they

they   they

they   They

They   They

Have your reader point to and read out loud each *they* on the next page.

Next, your reader will place the index card under the first sentence and begin reading. When the page has been read with three or less errors made, your reader is ready to continue to the next new sight word.

Reading lessons will be more effective if they take place when your reader feels the best. Is that in the morning, afternoon, or evening?

Refer to pages 11 and 12 for tips on correcting and/or repeating a page.

They see the .

They look up to see a 🇺🇸 .

They and she look up at the ☁️ .

He and they go to look for his ⚽ .

They and I look in the 🗄️ .

You and they look for a 🎃 .

They see that he is in his 🚗 .

They see that she was on a 🚜 .

They see that it was on the 🍳 .

They go to the ☂️ that was on the  .

Said

This page introduces the word *said*. Point to *said* below and say, "This is the word *said*." Point out the upper and lower-case letter *S* as needed. Now have the reader read the words on this page from left to right using the index card.

Said	said
said	Said
Said	said
Said	said
Said	said

Special Note: The sentences on the next page will contain quotation marks. Simply point out the quotation marks and say, "This is a quotation mark. There are quotation marks at the beginning and the end of what someone says. Quotation marks are used only when the *exact* words are being quoted, which is why some sentences have quotation marks, and some do not." Again – you are just making your reader aware of punctuation marks in the written language.

Have your reader point to and read out loud each *said* on the next page.

Next, your reader will place the index card under the first sentence and begin reading. When the page has been read with three or less errors made, your reader is ready to continue to the next new sight word.

Refer to pages 11 and 12 for tips on correcting and/or repeating a page.

They said to go on in the .

She said, "I see the  ."

He said, "Look for the and ."

"The 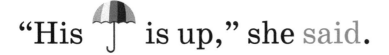 was in the ," she said.

They said to look up at the .

I said that a was on the .

"She looks up at the ," he said.

"His is up," she said.

You said, "It is for the ."

They said that he sees his on the .

With

This page introduces the word *with*. Point to *with* below and say, "This is the word *with*." Point out the upper and lower-case letter *W* as needed. Now have the reader read the words on this page from left to right using the index card.

With	with
with	With
with	with
With	With
with	With

Have your reader point to and read out loud each *with* on the next page.

Next, your reader will place the index card under the first sentence and begin reading. When the page has been read with three or less errors made, your reader is ready to continue to the next new sight word.

If your reader is struggling, begin another day
three to five sight words back.

Refer to pages 11 and 12 for tips on correcting and/or repeating a page.

They see the is with you.

Is that up in  with you?

That and go with the .

Was that the  with the ?

He was on the with a .

He said, "I see you with a ."

She sees a with a on it.

She looks for a with on it.

They said they see you with a .

He said for you to go in the with his

 and look at the .

Had

This page introduces the word *had*. Point to *had* below and say, "This is the word *had*." Point out the upper and lower-case letter *H* as needed. Now have the reader read the words on this page from left to right using the index card.

Had	had
Had	had
had	Had
had	Had
Had	had

Have your reader point to and read out loud each *had* on the next page.

Next, your reader will place the index card under the first sentence and begin reading. When the page has been read with three or less errors made, your reader is ready to continue to the next new sight word.

Refer to pages 11 and 12 for tips on correcting and/or repeating a page.

Was that the he had?

I see you had a with .

He had to look for a with a .

They said he had to go up in the .

He had a that was on the .

She said she had a at his .

Is that the you had?

They had it in the with a .

You had a at the ?

He had a and a on the .

Congratulations!

You have made it halfway through the 50 Sight Words!

For the last 25 words, your reader will now find the new colored sight words in the sentences and read them out loud starting from the top and reading down and then reading them up. After practicing the new sight words in this way, the reader can begin reading the sentences. As always, when the sentence page has been read with no more than three errors, your reader is ready to move to the next page.

Everything stays the same except that instead of reading the new sight word in a list, your reader is simply finding the new colored sight word in each sentence and reading them out loud.

Refer to pages 11 and 12 for tips on correcting and/or repeating a page.

All

All the 🧦 go in that 🗄️.

I see all his 📚 in the 📚.

He looks up at all the 🎈.

Look at all the 🍌 with the 🍇.

She had all the 🍅 in a 🍲.

You said to go with all the 🥧.

He had all the 🍬 on his 🛋️.

Is all that 🍕 for the 👦?

Was it all the 🍞 they had?

They said you had all the ✏️ and

all the 🖍️ with you.

Have

Look at all the I have.

She and he have a .

I have all the for the .

He said you have to go on a ?

I have had all the with a .

They have had to look at his .

I have to see the in the .

They have a that is up the .

I have a with a on the 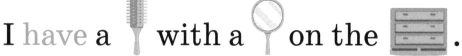.

She said that it was all they have in the with the .

Do

Do you have to look for  ?

Do you have all the ?

Do I look up at the ?

Do I go in his with on?

He and she do see the .

He said I had to do that for the .

Do they see it in the ?

He said they do have all the .

Do you see a that is in the ?

Was that all you had to do with the ?

Can

Can they see the ?

Can you go to look for the ?

He can have all the .

The can had all the in it.

He can look up with his .

You said the can I had is on a .

Can I do that with a and a ?

She looks at the can with .

Do they have a can for the ?

She can have the that was in the .

We

We do look at his .

We can all go with the .

She looks at the we have.

Do we go on the ?

I see we had all the .

They said that we can have .

Do we have to go on the  ?

We see the , and it is for you.

She said we can go up a .

He was in the that we had.

Be

We can all be in the  .

He can be on his .

Can you go to be with the ?

They had to be on that .

All his can be in the .

Do you have to be at the ?

Can we be in the and look up?

I said she was to be on the .

Is it to be for the ?

Do we have to be in the to see a

and a ?

Of

Do we have all of the  ?

All of the  can be in the  .

Do you have all of the 🍭 and 🍬 ?

He said she had all of the 🍞 .

All of the 👞👟 can be in a 🛍️ .

That was all of the 🌸 they had.

We have all of it with a 🥨 .

Go see all of the 🎨 I have for you.

All of the 🥘 is to go to that 🐱 .

We look up at all of his 🎃🎃🎃 on his 🚚 .

Not

She said it was not a .

We do not see all of the .

Is the with you and not the ?

They do not have to go to 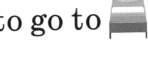 .

You and I have on, not .

All of that is not for you.

We can not be in that .

He can not be on the she had.

I look up at the , not the .

Not all of his can be in the .

There

They said a is not there.

There was a on his .

We can go there for a .

She said that the was not there.

The looks there for .

Do you have a in there?

All of it can not be there in a .

We look up there at all of the .

He had to be there with the .

I do see a and all of the  there.

78

What

What is it she can have in a ?

We look at what was on his 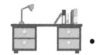.

What can the see up there?

A can not be what you see.

A is what can be there.

What is all of the for?

What can I have with all of the ?

What is there for the to do?

What can go with the and ?

He said that is not what they had

in the .

This

He had this with a .

This is what she had in a .

This is what we had for the .

This is what was on his .

They can go to this for it.

I look up at this and that .

Can this be all of the you have?

I can be on this , not the there.

Do you have this for his there?

We do not see the you said to look at

in this .

But

Special Note: Your reader has reached a point in the book where a sentence can be read without the use of pictures. Congratulate the reader!

I can see the but not a .

He is at this , but she is not.

They have , but I have .

What can this be but a ?

I had all of the but not a 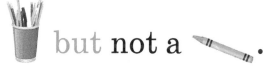.

Do you have this but not a ?

We go for all of it but not the .

I said to be there, but he was not.

She can go and look, but what can she see up there on that ?

I was in with a 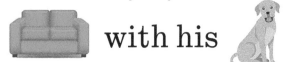, but he was on this 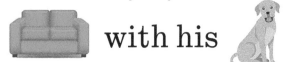 with his .

Are

I have 📚 that are for a 📚.

He said, "They are in the ⚪."

The 👡 she had are up there.

What I have in the 👜 are 🩴.

You are to go to the 🕐 to look at it.

You and I are to be with the 👶.

All of the 🍰 are to be on a 🪑.

He is on this 🚌, but we are not.

This 🧥 was there, but his 👓 are not.

See what you can do with the 🍴 that are

in this 🥘.

When

When can he and I see a ?

When do you have to be in ?

When are all of you up for ?

I was there but not when she was.

Look at his there when you can.

I had it when I was with the .

When are you on this ?

When can you look at what I have?

This is when she can have the but not the .

They said we can go when you look at what is in that .

One

It was there with one .

We can be there at one but not .

Go to this for one .

When can she look at one ?

He had one with all of his .

One is what I see when I look up.

What is one you do not have?

When can one be on the ?

They said that they are all on one  but not this .

She is in a , and they are all

in one .

Out

Special Note: Point out the exclamation marks and explain these are used to show strong feelings or a loud voice. Give an example and have the reader give an example. Have the reader point to all the exclamation marks.

When are you out with this ?

The is out!

Look out for one that is there!

Look at all of the out there!

Do you go out and up on this ?

What do you and he see out there?

When can we go out for ?

I can be out of a  but not in it!

She said his  are out!

They had to have 3  , but one was out!

Him

What 🏈 can be for him?

The 👶 looks up at him.

You have to go out with him for it!

She can look for his 🐕 with him.

We have 👖 but not one 👔 for him.

When do I go with him on a 🚲?

This is all of the 🍫 I had for him.

He said that they are with him.

One 🐒 was not in a 🌳, but with him

in this ⛺!

When the 👦 and 👧 are out there, they

can see him.

Some

Some of the are with him.

I had some when I was in bed.

She said one is in, but some are out!

Some of this can be for his .

I have some . What do you have?

Do you have some of that for him?

They said that some 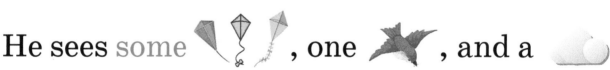 are on.

Some of it is for you to go and see!

He sees some , one , and a up there.

When can we look at some but not all of the out there?

As

As you can see, some  are out.

As for him, he can have some 🍩🍩 .

What do they do as they see him?

As a 👶 , I had a 🍼 but not a 🍥 .

When can she be there as a 👸 ?

As for the 🧍 , when is he on a 🏍️ ?

As he was in 🛏️ , a 🐶 was with him.

She can have all of it as I said.

As we go to the 🏚️ , we look at his 🚜

and that 🐄 .

One 🐈 is up this 🌳 as one 🐱 is out in

the 🌾 !

Were

When were some  in his ?

I see all of you were up on this !

He looks at the that were to go out,

but one is not there!

We were with one that was out.

We were there and had a for him.

As for the , what were they for?

She said 3  were to be it!

I do have some  that were his.

As for the , they were in a can.

Are there  that were for him?

Her

She looks at all of her 🌹 .

I can see a ⚪ for him and for her.

Some of her 👡 were not up there!

One is for her, but what is for him?

When can they look at her 🚲 ?

Do you have some of it for her?

As she was on her 🪑 , the 🧒 and 👧 were on this 🛋️ .

We are to be out of her 🛏️ , not in.

As for her, she can go out with you.

He said that he had his ✏️ on the 🗄️ with her 🖊️ .

Then

I was on the 🛹, then I was not.

I go with her and then have a 🥪.

Then can they look out of the 🪟?

Then he had some of it for him.

As I said, "Go see him and her, but then go on the 🚆 that is there.

As she sees the 🐸 and then some 🐟, a 🐰 looks at her.

What then can we do with all this?

When I have one 🍦, then we can go.

We were there then we were not!

Then you are to be up in his 🚁.

will

Will some of you go with her?

Were there , and will they go up?

Will there be some that were 🍅 ?

When will I see her and him?

As for him, he will go on the ✈ !

Will you then go to the 🗄 for it?

I said they had all his 🍬 but will not

have a 🎂 that was there.

As for her, she will look at the 📺 .

What will you do with this can?

We will then have one 🐷 that is out

when 3 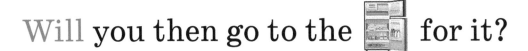 are in.

So

Look up so you can see that .

We were there, and so was a .

One is out, so then I will go and look

for all the in the .

So will some of you go with her?

As I said, "They are in the , so you

can be in it but not him."

So when were the to be for her?

So this is what she had at the ?

So do you see the as I look for it?

So then he was on his .

I have , so I can see a there!

From

He looks at a from his .

As I said, "It is for you from him."

She had on some from her .

I will go from this to see a !

So can you have the from there?

See a 🌼 and 🧁 that were from her.

From then on, we will all be in the ,

but we will not be with you.

From then on, all of the were in the

, so when was one out?

What I have from the are .

Do they go up there from the 🏠?

Let's Read a Story!

The next three pages are written in story form and provide practice for the last five sight words read.

Before beginning, have the reader read the last five new sight words on this page from left to right using the index card.

From	so
Will	Then
Her	from
then	will
So	her

Even though the next three pages are stories, the same method is followed. Have your reader place an index card under the first sentence and begin reading the story. When three or less errors are made on the story page, your reader is ready to move on to the next story page.

I will go from 🌳 to 🌳 to look for her 🐱 that is in one of the 🌲 up there. Then when I see the 🐱, I will go to the 🧍, and she will have her 🐱! So from then on, she will not have her 🐱 out, but will see that her 🐱 is in the 🏠. She will have 🥣 for the 🐱, so the 🐱 will not go out to look for 🥣.

The 🧒 looks at the 🐎🐎 from his

🪟. Do the 🐎🐎 have 🌾? He sees

that they do not have 🌾! Some 🌾 is

in the 🛖, so the 🐎🐎 will have 🌾

from there. The 🧒 will go from his 🏠

to the 🛖, and the 🐎🐎 will have

🌾. Then the 🧒 will go from the 🛖

to the 🏠, so he can look at the 🐎🐎

from his 🪟 and see they have 🌾.

He and she had a 🍦 from the 🗄, so the 🐕 had a 🍦 from the 🗄. He and she had a 🍰 from the 🎂 on the 🪑, so the 🐕 had some 🍰 from the 🎂 on the 🪑. He and she had a 🍕 from the 🔥, so the 🐕 had some 🍕 from the 🔥. Then he and she will go to 🛏, and so will the 🐕. Can they all have 🥞 when they are up from 🛏? They can!

They can all have 🥞 !

Way to go!
You've learned all
50 sight words!

Acknowledgments

A heartfelt thank you to the many parents who gave me the opportunity to help their sweet children become good readers - what a privilege! A special thank you to Traci Lovell and Barbie Mogle of Altoona Kidsworld 2 for allowing me to test my book out on their awesome kiddos. Another special thank you to Nicole Spaetzel for her suggestions and encouragement. A sweet thank you to my mother who taught me to treasure books. And a loving thank you to my husband, Mark, who always encourages me to pursue my work and ideas.

CPSIA information can be obtained
at www.ICGtesting.com
Printed in the USA
LVHW071109071221
705508LV00023B/500

9 781734 570700